CAT CARE
KW-064

CONTENTS

Overleaf: If given the proper care, your cat can be an active, happy pet. **Title page:** A shorthair cat, such as this one, will require less coat care than a longhair cat.

Photography: Isabelle Francais, Ron Moat, Fritz Prenzel, Ron Reagan, Reinhardt, Vincent Serbin, Skotzke & Lucas, A. Thies, Sally Anne Thompson, Louise Van Der Meid, Scott Van Duzor, Joan Wastlhuber.

© 1989 by T.F.H. Publications

Distributed in the UNITED STATES by T.F.H. Publications, Inc., One T.F.H. Plaza, Neptune City, NJ 07753; in CANADA to the Pet Trade by H & L Pet Supplies Inc., 27 Kingston Crescent, Kitchener, Ontario N2B 2T6; Rolf C. Hagen Ltd., 3225 Sartelon Street, Montreal 382 Quebec; in CANADA to the Book Trade by Macmillan of Canada (A Division of Canada Publishing Corporation), 164 Commander Boulevard, Agincourt, Ontario M1S 3C7; in ENGLAND by T.F.H. Publications Limited, Cliveden House/Priors Way/Bray, Maidenhead, Berkshire SL6 2HP, England; in AUSTRALIA AND THE SOUTH PACIFIC by T.F.H. (Australia) Pty. Ltd., Box 149, Brookvale 2100 N.S.W., Australia; in NEW ZEALAND by Ross Haines & Son, Ltd., 18 Monmouth Street, Grey Lynn, Auckland 2, New Zealand; in SINGAPORE AND MALAYSIA by MPH Distributors (S) Pte., Ltd., 601 Sims Drive, #03/07/21, Singapore 1438; in the PHILIPPINES by Bio-Research, 5 Lippay Street, San Lorenzo Village, Makati Rizal; in SOUTH AFRICA by Multipet Pty. Ltd., 30 Turners Avenue, Durban 4001. Published by T.F.H. Publications, Inc. Manufactured in the United States of America by T.F.H. Publications, Inc.

CAT CARE

DAGMAR THIES

Above: Outdoor cat runs can be set up anywhere, even, as here, in an urban backyard. **Facing page, top:** Cats love to play in high places. To prevent accidents, it is advisable to put mesh screening around your balcony if you allow your pet to play there. **Facing page, bottom:** This patient Cocker Spaniel is putting up with the cat kneading its back because of the long-standing friendship between them. A relationship such as this is not rare among pets, especially when both have been brought up together.

The Cat in Changing Times

The relationship between cat and man has changed innumerable times in the course of its almost 10,000-year history. Initially, the cat served purely as a practical animal, which, thanks to its hunting abilities, helped to protect human stores of food from mice and rats. It came and went when it pleased and took part in the domestic community at its own pleasure. It reproduced when it was time and independently reared its young in out-of-the-way places, only to bring them forward at its own discretion. It demanded nothing for its inestimable assistance. In many ways the cat still provides the same services today, either out in the countryside, thanked only with a saucer of milk, or in the backyards and cellars of cities, homeless and dependent on human compassion. Sometimes, however, the cat serves as a well-situated "employee" of a shop, restaurant or even an office.

When one considers that the "family cat" had already been portrayed in Chinese paintings during the first centuries of recorded history, the development of the cat in Western society into a true domestic animal proceeded very slowly. The course of the cat's "naturalization" suffered delays again and again when, in periods of war, it lived in want along with human beings, or when it was subjected to the most horrible persecution in its history approximately 500 years ago. A glorious period of the kind experienced in Egypt 5000 years ago, in which the cat enjoyed the highest honors of a god and was buried after its death in holy resting places, was never seen again.

Today the housecat serves as the "domestic animal of the future." Its popularity is steadily rising and the number of those who live with a cat is likewise steadily rising year by year— especially in the cities of the Western world.

The cat is unquestionably the cleanest, most aesthetic domestic animal we know. Its harmoniously flowing movements, various breeds, and bright color varieties fascinate everyone who has an eye for the naturally unadulterated. Its characteristic inclination toward humans confirms it as the ideal companion of those who are ready to understand it.

My heartfelt thanks to Dr. Hannahlore Schubert, whose ample experience as a veterinary doctor has contributed toward the creation of this book.

Facing page: A black male Persian. Double Champion Dulcie Jean's Sphiro of Geris. Owner, Geri Hamilton.

The face and paws of this lilac Burmese are distinctly darker than the rest of its body. Breeding the lilac color is closely related to the breeding of chocolate and blue. The eye color of the Burmese should be a rich gold.

A Tonkinese. "Tonks" are produced by mating Siamese with Burmese. Not all associations recognize the breed, although it is becoming popular with many cat lovers.

Buying a Cat

WHO SHOULD KEEP A CAT?

A cat cannot be made a slave. It takes its siesta when it needs rest, eats when it is hungry, and plays when it has rested enough. Therefore, it is not suitable as a plaything for children but perhaps as their acknowledged playmate. Often the best situation exists when the child and cat are allowed to grow up together. There are also children who are understanding enough to let the cat do as it likes. A cat can help others, by example, to rest and relax, thanks to its natural calm and harmony. This, however, must always be decided upon, according to circumstances, by the person rearing the cat.

For many childless couples, a cat becomes a welcome and cherished substitute for a child, and it helps the single person of all age groups to overcome loneliness and isolation with its playfulness, its longing for care and its unobtrusive tenderness. In this way the cat becomes an equal and understanding companion to one person and a "princess" in the house of another, who seeks to fathom its every wish so that it will never regret being with him.

None of us knows whether he is born to really be a cat lover, for the opportunity does not present itself in life to every potential cat lover to associate with cats. If he has preserved the objective enthusiasm for the animal in itself, then the first close relationship with a cat will surely fascinate him regardless of what type it is or from what lineage the cat comes. A cat neither lies nor deceives.

Even if a cat does not gladly leave its house because every corner and odor in it are familiar, a true domestic cat nevertheless feels at ease wherever its owner is. If the cat has the opportunity of getting to know the dangerous, deceptive freedom outside the house, however, and if it is tortured by children, chased by dogs or injured in traffic, then often it will regain its ease among people only with difficulty.

Many people are not capable of forming a relationship with a cat due to various, mostly subconscious, reasons and cannot control an often inexplicable discomfort in its presence. They often develop into outright cat enemies who, for all they care, would rather avoid a cat. It would be better for the cat lover to change his apartment rather than be forbidden from keeping a cat by such a landlord. A spouse, however, who, as a lover of animals, tolerates the acquisition of a cat without being an outspoken cat lover at first, will soon be among those who must quietly admit they are no longer able to live without one.

Facing page: A blue cream Persian. *Champion Reimars Puzzles of Insta-Purr. Owner, Marianne Lawrence.*

Above: This woman is holding a Seal Point Siamese. Note the darkness of its "points"—the ears, face, feet, and tail. When lifting a cat, the hind legs should be supported as well as the front legs and chest. *Facing page, top:* A piece of cardboard attached to the basket prevents these three-week-old kittens from making premature excursions around the house. *Facing page, bottom:* The difference between the sexes at ten weeks of age: the testicles of the male Seal Point on the right are already suggested by the elevated ridges beneath his anus. In comparison, the female Blue Point does not indicate these.

BUYING A CAT

HOW DOES ONE GO ABOUT GETTING A CAT?

There are many cat lovers who have this problem as soon as their secret dream, which for various reasons was not realized, is about to become reality. Having an occupation is not sufficient reason to deny one's desire for a cat, since the cat left alone all day is completely occupied with itself. In such cases the "two-child system," by which the cat lover provides his first housemate with a suitable younger playmate and living companion, is even more ideal. In any event, he should form a picture of the cat in his mind before seeking one, for it will be with him many years and therefore must suit him. Cats which have grown up healthy and are happy and content can live to an age of fifteen or more years!

If the dream of the cat lover is for a clever, obliging cat of unknown parentage to which he would gladly give a safe home, he might consider looking around in an animal shelter. Pet shops offer a variety of cats, from the purebred to the mixed breed, and these animals usually have some sort of health guarantee. He can also ask a veterinarian, who can probably assist him in finding a house-raised kitten or even a grateful full-grown cat. Newspapers also contain numerous offers through which he may easily get a delightful housecat of his choice. Perhaps this cat was an unplanned offspring which nevertheless was allowed to survive.

The cat lover who has always wanted a special breed of cat that shows a long line of ancestors and possesses a pedigree from a breeding association may at times find such a cat offered in the newspapers. Pet shops offer a variety of purebred cats. The possibility also exists of applying directly to a breeding association for addresses of serious cat breeders with whom one can correspond. The addresses of breeders are also published in hobbyist journals. Since it is well known that kittens only seldomly survive the stress of separation—in good health—from the mother and transport by train or plane in boxes or other containers, this type of transaction is often abandoned today. And it is just as well! Without the care of the responsible breeder who has lovingly raised the kitten in his home, further care may sometimes be a problem, especially during the first weeks following separation.

If a desirable kitten was discovered at a cat show, it would be better to allow at least two weeks to elapse before taking it home in order to determine whether it has gotten over the stress without becoming ill. A cat lover should therefore exercise patience and never take a cat home directly from a show.

A pair of Persian kittens at play. An important consideration for the prospective cat owner is the amount of grooming time that his pet will require.

If a long line of ancestors and everything that goes along with it is able to fill the cat lover with pride and joy, and if he is ready to gladly pay the appropriate amount for this prestige, he should not hesitate to buy a kitten of a particular breed. He should not, however, toy with the idea of breeding it himself. Along with a

Cats love the great outdoors, where they can explore their surroundings; however, it is safest to keep your cat indoors, away from dangers that may await it outside.

basic knowledge of breeding and heredity, substantially more is required than an inner love for cats.

CAT BREEDS

There are many excellent books in which the cat lover can obtain information about cat breeds in general and his own in particular so that he may share his home in untroubled harmony with a suitable cat. For this reason, the fundamental breed characteristics he should know will briefly be mentioned. Just as the outward appearance of cats gradually developed in a diverse manner through breeding, so did their separate identities change, but to a smaller degree. However, as in the case of human beings, just as little can be said regarding one race or the other which is of general validity. Even here exceptions are frequently the rule.

A cat lover who loves warmth and ease will probably be most compatible with a shorthaired cat whose fur lies flat on its body and shows hardly any short underfur. If, in addition, he requires a lively, playful, clever and gregarious companion which will play with him and miss no opportunity to show its devotion, then a member of the elegant slim breeds, such as the Siamese or Oriental Shorthair, is the right one for him. If, on the other hand, he loves the stout, full-bodied shorthair type with rounded head, short legs, plush soft hair richly lined with a short underfur (which seasonally sheds more than the other shorthair type), an even temperament and mellow little voice, he should select an American, European or even Exotic Shorthair. These cats are bred in many beautiful colors. On the other hand, he may be pleased by a cat with a medium build. This cat unites the characteristics of the first two breeds, and despite its stoutness, has an elegant effect, since its hair surrounds its body closely. Its disposition is mostly friendly, tranquil and placid. The Russian Blue, with its protecting thick hair, belongs to this group, as do the Burmese and Abyssinian.

The cat lover who longs for a

A windowsill in a warm, sunny location makes a comfortable perch for these short-hair tabby cats.

companion with long soft hair and a majestic appearance, a cat that outwardly rules over the house and welcomes its owner home with dignity and devotes its attention to him, should choose a Persian.

In addition, there are several intermediate forms whose silky hair is medium long and therefore relatively easy to care for. The Birman, with its four white paws, the whitish-red Turkish Van, the Balinese, and the Somali belong to this group. The "three-quarter Persian," usually called the "half-Angora," can also be considered in this group. Cats of the first hybrid generation, one of whose parents has long hair and the other short, rarely have hair longer than that of a British Shorthair. I would also like to mention here the slim cat breeds with curly hair, the Rex, and the tailless Manx and Cymric.

WHAT TO CONSIDER WHEN BUYING A CAT

After the cat lover has made his choice, he can make an arrangement with the seller of his future kitten to see it and perhaps bring it home immediately. If we are speaking of a housecat, he should make sure, if possible, that it is not younger than eight weeks and, better yet, that it is older than ten weeks. In nature, an independent mother cat cares for its young for several months before parting from them.

A kitten which is taken away too early is an orphan and experiences the same pains of separation as an orphaned child. In addition, at eight weeks and younger, the kittens are, naturally, not yet vaccinated. The cat lover should at this time make an appointment with the veterinarian to have his kitten examined, tested for worms, and vaccinated against the killer diseases.

The visitor to a breeder gets to see the mother and siblings of his kitten. It may also be possible for him to see the father and form a decent picture of his kitten's future body form. He will also see the surroundings in which the kitten grew, what type of litter it prefers to find in its litter box, where it likes to sleep, what room temperature suits it and what it plays with. If he is fortunate enough to observe the kittens at play, he can ascertain their state of health. A kitten that does not participate in play either does not feel well or has not had enough sleep. It is a good sign if all kittens are equally developed; male kittens might be a little larger than the females. It does not matter whether he chooses a male or female kitten because, even with cats, subsequent surroundings decisively influence further development, the most important factor being sensitivity!

When carefully lifted, a kitten should feel supple. The ribs, spine and pelvic bones should not be

Some people are happy in securing an adult cat—rather than a kitten—as a companion.

visible. The abdomen should be firm but not swollen, the skin smooth with soft shiny body hair neither clumped nor stuck together. Ears and eyes should show no secretions. In a word, a healthy, happy kitten smells pleasantly clean. At the age of ten to twelve weeks, breed characteristics begin to become evident, and the experienced breeder gradually begins to see which of the kittens will approach the ideal representation of the breed. If the cat lover is satisfied with his inspection, he should then buy the kitten.

A breeder cannot sell a kitten which has been carefully raised, wormed, and vaccinated without receiving remuneration.

The price is a matter of supply and demand and therefore varies in certain areas. The price of a purebred kitten depends upon the breed and color.

After the purchase (don't forget the receipt!), the seller provides papers, pedigree if purebred kittens, proof of vaccination, and a precise plan regarding present and future care. The seller can, in most instances, provide information regarding what to do with the kitten when it is not possible to take it on vacation. The cat lover should take pains to remain in contact with the seller, because very often subsequent problems regarding maintenance and care can be resolved through this contact.

Maintaining a Cat

The trip home in the carrying case can now be made. A thick layer of padding or newspaper forms the cushion. The breeder will surely lend a comfortable cloth to provide the kitten with a little home fragrance. If the trip home is not too long, the case will probably remain clean. If there is the possibility of taking the kitten out, it should be on a leash. If the trip home is in a closed case, the bars of the door must be small enough to prevent escape; a cloth must be placed in front of the door to protect the inside from fluctuations in temperature caused by drafts. Drafts are as dangerous to cats as they are to humans. Carrying bags are impractical, since there is a problem of getting an excited cat into one while simultaneously manipulating the zipper. Besides, the smooth insides very quickly become moist from the kitten's breath. The cages specially developed by the airlines for animal transport are made of high-impact plastic and are fitted with mesh doors. Condensation cannot form in them as in a cat case. One must only be careful that the mesh door faces to the rear, especially on drafty train platforms. Such a cage, fitted with a soft washable cloth and raised a bit, serves as pleasant quarters for the cat at home and at the same time becomes a place in which the cat feels safe and secure on trips.

So many new impressions assault the kitten's senses after its final departure from mother, siblings, erstwhile keeper, and trusted surroundings that its entire being is filled with tension. However, it gradually calms down and listens as it is tenderly and softly spoken to. A healthy curiosity gradually awakens. If the kitten is alone with the driver, it is best if he leaves the kitten in its house next to him on the front seat. The kitten can then see and listen to him until it falls asleep. One thing is important: windows and convertible tops are to remain closed during the trip, since the cool air circulating in the car can easily have the effect of a draft.

If there is another passenger in the car, the cat should sit next to him in its house on the back seat. He can let the kitten smell his hand, open the door and tenderly caress it as soon as it calms down. When the inside of the car is warmed, he can place the collared and leashed kitten on his lap when he notices a soft purring. But please be careful and do not let go of the leash. The kitten can easily climb onto the driver's shoulder, jump on his lap and, perhaps most unfortunate of all, land under the gas or brake pedal before it can be prevented. It is

Facing page: A characteristic trait of all cats is their penchant for cleanliness. At its young age, this kitten already knows the basics of good grooming.

advisable to place a box of kitty litter between front and rear seats on long trips. The kitten (on its leash) should be able to easily reach it.

Almost all trips with cats proceed in the same manner. When using the railroad, do not sit in the direction of travel, because of drafts, if you wish to hold your leashed cat on your lap. A kitten will, of course, weather a trip without danger in a carrying case. It is important to see that the case's air holes always remain unobstructed, especially when it must be placed on the luggage rack. If possible, a kitten should make airline trips in the passenger compartment alongside its keeper.

Contrary to popular belief, cats and dogs are not "natural enemies."

"Cat in cabin" must be requested in advance since only a certain number of animals are allowed in the passenger compartment. During a turbulent flight, the door to the transport cage or lid to the carrying case should be opened a little to softly and tenderly hold the kitten steady and prevent it from unexpectedly hitting the cover or sides.

Due to great temperature fluctuations, flights in the luggage compartment are not recommended. Moreover, a cat's hearing is so sensitive that the droning engines may cause it to suffer unforgettable shock. This can have an inordinate effect years after the fact, should another trip be made.

Motion sickness is rare in cats. To avoid it, the cat's last meal should be at least five hours before departure. Sedatives and drugs for motion sickness should be prescribed only by a veterinarian, since cats react to them differently than do humans or dogs.

When her kittens are weaned, this mother cat will be able to catnap to her heart's content.

ARRIVAL AND THE NEW HOME

Immediately after the first trip, the cat lover should become a substitute mother for his new housemate. He should not endanger this budding relationship of trust and should therefore place the kitten back in its house just before reaching home. It would be outright dangerous to cross the street with the kitten in one's arms. A young kitten can be injured should it attempt to free itself to reach a secure haven when it is suddenly frightened. For this reason, the kitten should be made to feel secure about moving into its new home. It

should be as peaceful as possible during these crucial moments of moving in. The sounds of playing children, loud laughter, scolding speech, and slamming doors would be negative impressions which the kitten would surely perceive. The kitten's cage or basket should be placed in a quiet, protected corner of a warm room, preferably on the floor near a heating duct. The mesh door should be slowly opened while soft, encouraging words are spoken, allowing the kitten to look around and get to know its new domain. The kitten should then be allowed to do as it pleases. Children should not be permitted to run after it.

A stable earthenware or porcelain water-filled dish resting

A tortoiseshell-and-white longhair.

on a bright tray should be nearby. A bright (it is said that cats love red), steady plastic or enamel litter box should be next to the little house. The kitten is familiar with its contents. Cat litter is preferable to all other materials. The size of the box should be about 16×12 inches.

The room should be set up with a suitable toy and a scratching or climbing post. Some favored toys are a round wicker basket in which the kitten can rock itself or roll around in when it wishes, a cardboard carton suitable for playing and hiding, a long piece of twine, knotted at the end and hanging from the ceiling, a solid, brightly colored rubber ball, chestnuts or nuts for rolling and pushing, a cork, and a crumpled piece of paper. Objects which are too small and made of soft plastic are unsuitable because of the danger of their being swallowed.

The kitten needs a companion who will instill confidence and replace its missing mother and siblings. It is advantageous, therefore, not to leave the kitten alone the first night and to permit it a further view of its new home only after use of the litter box and a healthy appetite indicate that it has gotten used to its new surroundings. Some time should be spent with the kitten encouraging it to capture, hunt and climb to avoid homesickness. The cat lover, however, must immediately seek advice from the

This kitten, a tortoiseshell-and-white shorthair, is fascinated by a simple object: a piece of ribbon.

seller if, after three days, the kitten still shows no signs of hunger or if it declines its favorite foods as prescribed in the feeding plan. Continued refusal of food can critically weaken a kitten's body defenses and cause it to become so ill that only a veterinarian will be able to help it. The kitten should be brought back to its mother for a week or two if there is no immediate change in the condition despite all pains

taken to resolve the problem. When it once again moves into its new house, what was once new will be familiar and its further development should proceed without difficulty.

HOUSEMATES WITH PREVIOUS RIGHTS

An established cat in a household expects respect from the new arrival. The future relationship depends upon the

A scratching post like this one is an excellent device upon which a cat can exercise its claws. If your pet forgets the house rules and starts clawing on furniture or drapes, give it a firm verbal "No," and immediately escort it to the scratching post for a refresher lesson.

results of an ancient "ceremony" which will unfold between them should the intruder into its domain also be a confident individual. It begins with a majestic, impressive posturing, ears laid back, hair bristling, followed by sudden attacks by one and flight and defense by the other. These are underscored by sirenlike sounds and awful screeching. A bitter duel takes place between male cats, with attacks by both opponents. A milder stage of the ritual consists mostly of deep growling. Through the performance of this ritual, domination is dispelled; peaceful coexistence will begin soon after.

The cats will have to be separated, however, if this gradual diminution of the reaction between the cats is not observed and if behavior remains unchanged over several days. There is hardly any danger of this being necessary if the new housemate is a young kitten, since the first two phases of

the "ceremony" are mostly symbolic. After a while, the older cat approaches the intruder and it lies on its side, its defensive weapons ready, ears back and growling softly. The older cat now draws back discreetly and excites the curiosity of the kitten. It hops on stiff little legs after the other, impressively posturing with hair bristling. The older cat now growls and spits at the kitten. The cat

Some cats enjoy the security of a hooded basket.

lover can hasten the acquaintance of the two from this point on by pacification and petting. Animosity between the cats can be dispelled by lightly sprinkling them with the same fragrance, such as cologne.

One should never lose patience. The course of the ritual should in no case be interrupted by well-meant separation of the two. Every interruption forces the ritual to begin all over again! The situation is different when a dog meets a cat as housemate for the first time. Success in acclimating the two is often only promising when the kitten is young and inexperienced. A dog which has never before encountered a cat must become accustomed to its smell. As long as the kitten is not present, the dog may be allowed to inspect its room after two or three days. Meanwhile, the kitten should be allowed to investigate the dog's area. Because the kitten may defensively swipe at the dog with its paw, attention should be given to seeing that the leashed dog does not approach the kitten too closely at their first meeting. Within a few days, the distance between them may be reduced during their short meetings with

Quadruple Grand Champion Beverly-Serrano Petite, a chinchilla silver Persian. Owners, Mr.and Mrs. E.W. Peterson.

Kissame Hard To Be Humble of Hexham, cream-and-white male Rex. Owner, K. Dale Baer.

petting and encouragement. Dogs are primarily interested in the smell of the rear parts of their species, which is indelibly impressed upon them. Cats mostly prefer nasal contact. The owner acts here as an understanding intermediary between the two different creatures. The dog will gladly and willingly accommodate its owner's wishes and happily accept the new housemate into the family if it unreservedly recognizes the owner as master. Close friendships between dogs and

A calm environment is important for the mother cat and her nursing babies. Pictured is a blue-and-cream longhair with blue longhair and cream longhair kittens.

cats are not rare. A dog frequently forms a life-long association with its first cat companion. If the cat should die, the dog will tolerate its successors, but the relationship between him and them will never be as close as that with the first cat.

There is very little chance that a cat that has had negative experiences with dogs will become a companion to a dog having no positive experiences with cats. On the other hand, raising a dog and a cat together from the time they are young usually presents no difficulties. White mice, hamsters, guinea pigs, and rabbits must, by their nature, unavoidably tolerate a kitten as a new housemate and will, for the most part, be accepted by the kitten. As a rule, large parrots soon gain the kitten's respect. To avoid unforeseen incidents, however, a kitten should only be allowed in their presence under a watchful eye.

Small birds should be spared the sight and presence of cats of

...From T.F.H., the world's largest publisher of bird books, a new bird magazine for birdkeepers all over the world...

CAGED BIRD HOBBYIST
IS FOR EVERYONE
WHO LOVES BIRDS.

CAGED BIRD HOBBYIST
IS PACKED WITH VALUABLE
INFORMATION SHOWING HOW
TO FEED, HOUSE, TRAIN AND CARE
FOR ALL TYPES OF BIRDS.

Subscribe right now so you don't miss a single copy! SM-316

any age, since they become too excited. A cat will often sit for hours in front of an aquarium, watching the colorful fish as they swim back and forth. The kitten should not have the opportunity, however, to fish for them. The aquarium should be carefully covered, allowing enough room for fresh air to enter. This pleasantly warming and amusing resting spot will soon become the kitten's favorite place.

Persian cats are known for their flowing, luxurious coats.

HOUSEHOLD DANGERS

A lively kitten participates in all household and familiar events. It keeps track of the smallest changes in its surroundings. Nothing escapes its attention—no new picture, nail, pencil, or needle on the floor (which is especially dangerous when threaded). The kitten truly has an educational influence on its keeper, because he must always think about not leaving anything around which could be swallowed out of curiosity during play and necessitate an operation. The following objects are dangerous:

rubber bands, rubber mats, erasers (rubber provokes biting), string, yarn remains, any form of tobacco (nicotine is poisonous), matches and match boxes, small balls of foil (candy wrappers), childrens' toys made of soft plastic, plastic bags (danger of suffocation), glass beads and buttons, fragments of glass and earthenware, as well as all kinds of medication not intended for the kitten.

As pleasant as it is to decorate an apartment with plants, some plants can be poisonous to the kitten when eaten and cause serious reactions (sudden loss of appetite, frothing at the mouth, vomiting of green foam, sometimes diarrhea, rarely fever). A house-raised kitten lacks the instinctive ability to distinguish between poisonous and non-poisonous plants. It frequently finds water from a vase especially tasty, although this can be dangerous. For this reason, cut

A tortoiseshell Oriental Shorthair. It is not unusual for a cat to sit up on its hind legs when something captures its attention.

A pair of Persian cats. Their long hair must be carefully brushed and combed each day in order to keep them looking their best.

flowers should be just as unreachable to the kitten as the following plants: arum plants such as anthurium, scindapsus (ivy), philodendron, all types of evergreens, orchids, spurge plants (including poinsettia), geraniums (pelargonium), bulb plants of all types (tulip, hyacinth, scilla, narcissus), lily of the valley, foxglove, laburnum, vetch, solanaceae (nightshade) and, because of their needles, cactus.

Cleaning materials are another source of danger. Those which contain phosphates cause blood poisoning.

All cats are fascinated by the crackling of suds and drops of water attendant when doing the wash. To preclude the cat's ingesting such materials by licking its paws, it should be excluded from the laundry room. The same holds true when the floor is being washed. It would be more appropriate and hygienic if, when washing the floor, a harmless disinfectant were used. In general, whatever is harmful to a child is harmful to a kitten.

Because a kitten can ingest them when caring for its hair, sprays of all kinds, spot removers, all tar products, turpentine, moth balls, furniture polish, and wet paint are poisonous.

Leaps from curtains and high furniture which can lead to broken bones can be easily avoided if the kitten is taken down by its keeper. A kitten sometimes does these things intentionally when it feels neglected by its master and wishes to be held. There is a danger of head injuries from heavy objects which are easily tipped. A kitten, like a child, does not recognize the dangers posed by fire, heaters and electricity. Before unpleasant accidents occur, measures should be taken to prevent them. Electrical wires should be hidden and electrical outlets and heaters covered. Caution should be exercised with hot irons, boiling liquids and heating pads. The list is certainly not complete, however. The more important dangers can be avoided when they are known. Open windows also pose a danger; it would be better to air a room when the kitten is not in it or, better yet, when it is in its little house, protected from drafts. A

A Russian Blue and her kittens. Members of this cat breed have plush double coats.

Pet-quality or show-quality, cats can be wonderful household companions.

veterinarian should be sought immediately should an accident or poisoning occur despite all precautions.

CONTROLLING THE URGE FOR FREEDOM

The observation that a cat is a freedom-loving creature is certainly true. This does not mean, however, that the cat should be allowed unrestricted freedom. Experience shows that the home in which a cat lives is quite sufficient to satisfy its desires for movement and change. Many dangers await the cat outside, and a responsible cat lover will see to it that the cat is never allowed outside unaccompanied. Only in a few areas today can a cat live to 12 or more years out in the open. The greatest age, unfortunately, is hardly more than two to five years. The most frequent cause of death, next to shooting (of an ostensibly "wild" animal) or endemic rabies, is death in traffic, followed by poisonings of all kinds (chemical, fertilizers, and insecticides ingested by licking paws as well as ingestion of poisoned small animals) and infectious diseases, primarily panleukopenia. Parasites—ticks, fleas, worms, and mites—pose another danger. Besides, there can easily be uncontrolled and uninhibited reproduction of free-roaming cats.

The cat owner should be aware

of the sexual maturation of his pet. A female kitten often begins to roll lustfully on the floor, lick herself constantly, and raise her back forcefully against one's hand during petting at the age of about seven months. She is in heat! She calls loudly and longingly for a partner, especially at night. After a week, the uproar disappears but is repeated, independent of seasonal changes, at irregular intervals. The drive to escape is dangerous at this time.

A young male cat has the same powerful drive for a female cat when it becomes sexually mature. He also becomes restless, sings "love songs" loudly and demandingly, and marks with a lasting scent the most prominent places in his domain to entice a female. During this time both male and female develop an astonishing gift for discovery: they learn how door handles are depressed (these can be turned upside down to prevent the door from being opened) and how windows which are opened a bit are raised. They steal away from balconies and climb over rooftops, returning home, after days of being gone, in pitiful condition. Some cats never make it home at all.

There is only one solution to this problem for both the male and the female cat—surgical removal of the gonads. Since the accompanying manifestation of heat in cats (marking in males,

estrus in females) is unpleasant to people, complete castration is preferred, as a rule, over sterilization (where the function of the gonads remains). A veterinarian performs the operation on the narcotized animal. The cat lover can usually take his housemate home the same day. Experience has shown that the operation is only successful when the reproductive organs are fully developed. The minimum age to neuter a male cat is at about nine or ten months, after he has begun to "mark." For females it is about one to one and one-half years, but never before the first pronounced estrus. Older male and female cats can also be castrated without injury. This prevents uncleanliness, inordinately strong desires for freedom, and unwelcome offspring. If a female kitten appears too delicate for such an operation, it can be postponed by using the "pill" as prescribed by a veterinarian. Should the female's constant companion be an as yet uncastrated male, the pill should be given once a week. It can be used to reduce the intensity of estrus until the kitten is ready for the operation. During this time,

Facing page: *Double Champion Du-Ro-Al's Gorgeous George of Nephrani, a male Somali. Owners, Ruth and Bob Morris.*

half a tablet should be given on the day following estrus, and a half the day after that. Every case is different and requires renewed consideration; there is usually no use for the pill with cats intended for breeding. After the operation, both male and female cats are playful, well behaved and as content as before while enjoying all the comforts of home.

LEASH AND CAT RUN

There is usually no problem in getting a kitten used to a collar or harness and leash. It often learns to walk on a leash with no problems. A cat becomes accustomed to frequent auto trips relatively quickly, and there is no problem in taking it out to the countryside for some fresh air and a change of scenery. To prevent infection, one should have himself vaccinated against tetanus, and in any case have the cat vaccinated against rabies. The trip for the cat would better be made in its usual house. Do not forget it when getting out! The house provides the best refuge from unpleasant and painful incidents, should it suddenly rain or should there be some unexpected danger. When resting, the cat should be tied by its leash to its house. To allow the kitten sufficient room for movement, the leash should not be too short. Kittens have a predilection for climbing, and should a kitten climb a tree, the leash provides an easy way to get

it to come down.

As a cat becomes older, it begins to lose pleasure in such exhausting excursions. It feels more comfortable and protected in its usual surroundings. The cat lover should, therefore, consider another means of providing fresh air and sunshine. In the city, of course, he will be able to use one of the means suggested here. In this case, the cat's feeling of security need never be disturbed.

A window box can be constructed as a look-out for the cat, should living in the city provide no better possibilities. The cat can be allowed to sun itself here on warm summer days protected from drafts. A wooden frame can be covered with wide meshed screening. Regular screening is not suitable, as the cat can get caught up in it with its claws and seriously harm itself. This frame box can be either hung on hinges or placed securely in the window in such a manner as to allow them to open and close easily.

Another possibility is a built-in roofed porch, the front of which can easily be covered with wide-meshed wire or plastic screening hung securely on the wall with hooks. In general, such balconies should be so devised as to prevent accidents, since cats, in their eagerness to catch a flying insect or bird, may easily jump, fall out, lose their balance and fatally injure themselves. Cats are not

A blue-and-white longhair enjoying a moment of rest and solitude.

always as adroit as they are often made out to be!

A sunny balcony to an apartment may also be covered with wire mesh screening, allowing birds which enter an easy escape. The upper half of the balcony door should also have wide mesh screening fastened securely to the outside frame. The side walls can be covered with a tightly meshed plaiting; flower boxes can serve as a windbreak. They can contain grass for the cat, which can be cut and watered like normal grass, or non-poisonous decorative flowers such as nasturtium or marigolds. A quick-dry straw mat can cover the floor. A piece of twine with pieces of paper attached and the cats usual house containing a warm blanket complete the layout. The cat lover can now leave the balcony door open even in his absence without any concern. The temperature in the shade should measure at least 15°C (59°F). At the onset of cooler evening temperatures, the outer door to the balcony should be closed, since every cat is fascinated by the happenings outside and as a rule fails to come in. If the cat lover owns his own home and is not bound to strict rules concerning construction as is an apartment dweller, there are many other ideas for cat runs which he can use to the benefit of his cat.

A large cat kennel, about six feet high, with a climbing post, resting places on a balcony, platform, or grass can be constructed near the family area. This cat run must also be roofed with a wide mesh screening. Experience shows that even a three-foot wide horizontal overhang of the walls is usually not sufficient to prevent a cat from climbing out. Many breeders use an electrified fence. A special wire is fitted by means of insulators inside the garden or cat run. The fence should be at least three feet high. Only cats which have lived in complete freedom will be able to hurdle this fence. Glass walls of about six feet do not necessarily require further escape-preventive devices. There are cat specialists, however, who do recommend such devices.

All these layouts should be easily accessible through windows or doors from the common living quarters. Access to the garden should be made through an escape run or transfer chamber to prevent inadvertent escape of the cat when entering or leaving the cat runs. A sunloving cat will be satisfied with a home-built hanging balcony, should the area in front of a ground floor window be insufficient to permit construction of a roomy ground-reaching cat run. This can also be furnished simply and suitably with a resting place, grass and mat. Cat runs should not be accessible to strange people, children and dogs, so that the cat may use it in undisturbed peace.

MOVES AND VACATIONS

Because of the accompanying stress, every move from one residence to another is unpleasant to all parties concerned. This excitement is transferred to the four-legged housemates unless they are shielded from the turmoil by the cat lover. The most intelligent thing to do would be to completely clear a room in the old residence before packing begins in the other rooms. The cat's usual basket or case is placed in this empty room. For comfort, the cat should be left its litter box, water dish, toys and perhaps a small piece of carpet. The room should then be closed and left off-limits to movers.

The procedure in the new apartment is reversed; the bathroom is furnished with its usual furniture and the cat, together with its house, is placed in its most quiet corner. Afterwards the cat is allowed to inspect the room. If it is satisfied, the door should be closed and the room will serve as a peaceful island in the midst of confusion. The small housemate, regularly consoled and pacified, should be allowed inspection of the other rooms only when moving is completed.

There should be no difficulties in acclimatization, since basically only the external aspects of the rooms have changed, not the contents, and the family has remained the same.

Vacations and trips with a cat proceed according to the same principle: a cat can tolerate changes more easily if it is with a person it trusts. A cat will feel more at home if it is accustomed to the car in which it will be traveling. If its own home is at its disposal, it will have no occasion to feel unhappy in strange places. The scale of a cat's feelings can range from deepest dejection, when it feels neglected by its keeper, to the feeling of extreme comfort.

There are several things one should never forget when traveling with a cat. The most important are the traveling cage, its house, collar and leash, a bottle of fresh

The Cat-A-Lac from Designer Products is sturdy and durable and folds easily for storage.

water from home so that it may adapt along the way, canned food (since one never knows where he may get fresh meat), food additives (vitamins, pure yeast, condensed milk), can opener, spoon and knife, eating and drinking containers, everything for care of the hair, a warm blanket, good leather gloves, first aid kit, 70% alcohol, litter box and litter. Information should be obtained from the responsible government authorities regarding customs requirements for animals when trips abroad are intended. There must be proof of vaccination against rabies at least four weeks prior to the trip. Re-vaccination against enteritis is also mandatory.

A suitable shelter for the cat should be found should the possibility exist of the trip being too fatiguing, because of its length or uncertainty of lodgings; it would be better to change one's vacation plans for the cat's sake! The best solution would be to leave it alone in the apartment during the vacation. This realization has led in the past few years to an entirely new part-time job for those who remain at home—cat-sitting. A reliable friend, neighbor or acquaintance could be asked, with the promise of remuneration, to visit the apartment regularly, mornings and evenings, to provide the cat with food, water, new litter and, of course, sufficient petting. At the same time, the apartment

could be checked to see that all is OK. Always leave your vacation address behind. The cat lover can then return home refreshed to a likewise well-rested cat.

A vacation spot must be found for the cat if it is not possible to find a cat-sitter. The prerequisites are that the cat be completely healthy, wormed and, once again, vaccinated against enteritis and rabies so far as this is possible. To facilitate acclimatization, the cat's stay in strange surroundings should be spent in its own house with its own blanket. The more the cat sees things it is accustomed to, the better it will overcome the pain of separation. It is advisable, at first, to contact the breeder. The breeder can sometimes suitably lodge and carefully tend to the cat for compensation. The cat may not readily recognize him, particularly if it is not permitted to live in the room in which it was raised. After a few days, however, the spell is broken, and a cat can often get used to an otherwise strange play companion (prerequisite—castration) for the duration of its stay. The days and weeks in strange surroundings usually pass quickly for these trusting companions because they can mutually divert and console each other. The breeder may often be able to suggest a suitable cat lover in his stead should late vacation planning exclude him as a possible alternative.

The most doubtful and

Give love and attention to your cat and you will have a warm and lasting friend. Pictured is a lilac Oriental Shorthair.

dangerous manner for a cat to spend a vacation is being boarded in a large, overcrowded animal shelter amidst the noise of barking dogs. This is usually done hastily as a last resort before the trip. It would be better, of course, not to take such a vacation. Even here, the cat should hopefully inhabit its own house, but the comfort and care which it needs to overcome its anxiety is usually lacking. Because of the noise and confusion, older cats especially, and perhaps even those left alone for the first time, often reject food for days. Bodily functions do not proceed properly under stress. To preserve its health, there remains only one way out: getting home quickly! A cat has difficulty overcoming negative experiences. The concern of the cat lover should therefore be to spare his cat these experiences as much as is possible. It behooves the cat lover to carefully and responsibly plan his vacation in advance so that it may be unforgettable for him and, on the other hand, quickly forgotten by his cat.

Caring for a Cat

LIFTING, CARRYING, AND PACIFYING

A mother cat fastens onto the hair at the neck to lift and carry its young. Pressure on certain nerves triggers carrying immobility, which causes the kitten to hang limply with drawn-in hindpaws and stretched-out forepaws. The kitten is carried in this manner—without struggling or crying—up to a certain age. When the kitten is grown, however, carrying by the mother ceases.

In picking up his kitten, the cat lover should not carry or grab hold of it in this manner. Instead, he should draw close to it slowly and quietly bend down (cats love being played with at their level). The cat is then allowed to sniff his hand and is encouragingly stroked on the back. He then takes hold of the cat with one hand under the ribcage, surrounding its forepaws with his fingers, and lifts its body with the other under the rear paws. To carry the cat he simply places it on his hip, holding on to its forepaws and nestling it in the crook of his arm. The other hand pets and holds its head to comfort and divert it. Even very large cats are carried from their cages and through crowds in this manner by show attendants. Very young kittens can be carried against the breast, as they do not yet have the strength to attempt freeing themselves. Veterinarians must sometimes use other holds to prevent violent defensive

reactions from excited cats. These holds, however, only concern those keepers who know their animal and its reactions.

There are cats which do not allow themselves to be either picked up or carried. In most cases, however, such cats can, with encouragement, be directed without problems into a transport cage. A cat shocked by terror or fear should be allowed to settle down before it is handled. This is usually the case when a cat is found in a hiding place or up a tree after panic-stricken flight. No attempt should ever be made to pursue, capture, or even touch a panic-stricken cat. Severe injuries could be the unavoidable consequences of such carelessness.

Similar situations arise for example when two rival male cats fight. If it is not possible to separate them by forcing one from the room, throwing a heavy blanket on one or both of them will help. The cats can then be separated, during the ensuing pause in their fighting, by using the blanket. Never handle a terrified cat with unprotected hands—even leather gloves offer no protection. Leave it alone and then softly speak to it. Allow it to sniff your hand as a test, and only

Facing page: The Persian cat's nose is short and broad. This cat is owned by José Langevin.

then place a comforting hand on its back, pet it, hold it, and lift it. Never forget the collar and leash when transporting a cat out of doors.

CARE OF EYES AND EARS

Except when there is injury or sickness, only the skin and ears require special care. Care of the eyes is usually not necessary. A veterinarian should be consulted if a secretion of mucus or pus is discovered at the corners of the eyes. Before he can treat it properly, his task is to discover its cause (infection? blockage of tear or nasal ducts? foreign bodies in the eyes? injury?). Washing the eyes with boric acid, which is often suggested, can only lead to irritation and should, therefore, not be attempted.

The ears should be wiped once a week with a boric acid salve or baby oil and a cotton swab. Take care to hold the cat securely. Dust and normal secretions are easily cleaned away in this manner. Consult a veterinarian if you are given the care of a kitten which lays its ears back, reacts irritably when one creeps behind it, shakes its head frequently, and shows blackish-brown crusty secretions in its ears when closely observed. He will be able to recommend proper treatment once the underlying cause is determined. Once the symptoms remit, regular care can prevent a recurrence of the illness.

The most extensive of a cat's sense organs is its skin which is cared for by the cat, along with its hair.

CAT CLEANLINESS

A cat spends its time lavishly preening, massaging, washing, combing, and brushing its hair when it is not sleeping, playing, or eating. Because prey in nature would catch its scent, a cat's instinct does not allow it to tolerate its own odor. A housecat strictly maintains this instinctive behavior, although its prey consists, at most, of a toy or its food.

As soon as a cat is petted with hands smelling of soap or cremes, the process promptly starts all over again. A mother cat washes, cleans, and massages its kittens several times a day. To encourage digestion, the abdomen is licked by her coarse tongue until it is gorged with blood and pinkens. At the same time, the kitten is cleaned of its excrement. The mother cat often unaccountably nibbles off the kitten's seemingly annoying whiskers when caring for its hair.

A kitten begins to show an interest in the litter box at an age of about three weeks in its endeavor to keep itself absolutely clean and odor free. The kitten at first seems to think of the litter box's contents as food. At this age it is still kept clean by its mother, but soon it sits in the typical cat manner. It does not take long

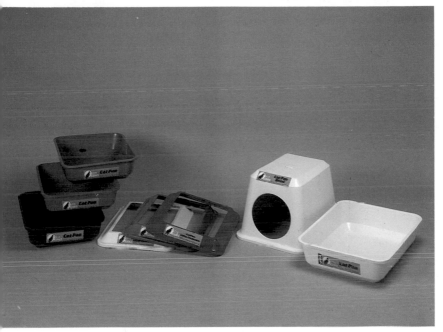

Hagen's Cat Pan and Hood, which comes in a number of attractive colors, is lightweight and easy to clean.

before the kitten begins to carefully cover up its products with its forepaws. The kitten retains this behavioral characteristic throughout its life. Nothing is more offensive to a kitten than a filthy litter box. For this reason, a kitten will consistently avoid using such

a litter box and will seek a soft blanket or other suitable place when necessary. This does not mean the kitten is dirty but rather that it is extremely fastidious. Therefore, the cat lover should regularly empty, wash, dry and refill the litter box mornings, evenings, and even during the day when necessary. A harmless disinfectant should be used once a week when cleaning the box.

There may also be a psychological reason for a cat's

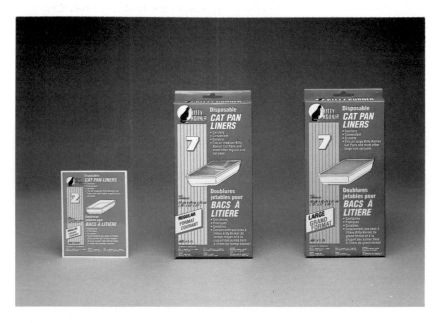

Cleaning the litterbox is made easy with Hagen's Cat Pan Liners, which are available in several sizes.

uncleanliness such as isolation, neglect and/or jealousy. In this case, the causes must be determined and eliminated. Only neutering will help an unsatisfied sex drive.

A healthy cat will begin cleaning itself at an age of two or three weeks. It executes the most peculiar acrobatic maneuvers in reaching the furthermost parts of its body. A full-grown cat finds cleaning its throat to be most difficult. It brushes its face, eyes, ears, and neck thoroughly, using the constantly licked soft fur of its forepaws. A sign of affection and closeness among several cats living together is indicated when there is mutual grooming to help clean difficult-to-reach parts of the body.

It is not uncommon for hairs to get into the cat's stomach during this intensive cleaning procedure. Since hair is indigestible, it forms hairballs or clumps which are, from time to time, eliminated. A free-roaming cat eats grass to make this regurgitation easier. A housecat should be offered wide-leaved, stiff grass with a rough edge or sowed oats. Small boxes of ready-to-eat grass can be bought in a pet shop.

Cyperas, however, is most favored because it has the regurgitative properties of stiff grass. This plant, obtained from a gardener, should be inspected to be certain it has not been treated with insecticides. It is a decorative house plant and could be placed in an inaccessible room, regularly watered and fertilized, and could occasionally be offered to the cat.

A longhair cat has difficulty caring for itself, and its own body care is mostly symbolic. This type of cat should be assisted in its own care to prevent it from swallowing too many hairs and to make it easier for yourself when cleaning carpets and furniture.

CARING FOR THE CAT'S HAIR

A cat's fur is composed of several types of hair which have developed differently according to breed. It usually consists of equally distributed protective hairs, which, in turn, are composed of separate, compact sleek hairs. The undercoat is formed more or less of dense woolly or downy hairs.

In the Siamese, Oriental Shorthair and Burmese cats, this undercoat is the sparsest. For this reason, the protective hair lies close to the body and acts as a smooth shiny second skin. Shedding is always taking place but it is hardly noticeable. In caring for the fur, it should be stroked vigorously once a week with clean, moist hands until they are dry. Loose hairs will remain on your hands. A moist chamois or rubber brush can also be used, but caution is advised so as not to remove live hairs. Brushing is unpleasant to many cats and they become uneasy, probably because of the static electricity generated. After brushing, a fine-toothed, blunt comb should be used and the hair carefully and thoroughly combed to massage the skin and remove loose fur.

The cat's entire coat, including abdomen, is brushed with a dry brush and smoothed by hand to complete the job. The coat's wonderful lustre is thereby maintained, and cats cared for in this manner always look good regardless of the time of year.

The other shorthair breeds usually have a dense undercoat. Their fur therefore projects a bit from the body. The undercoat is shed during spring and grows again in fall after the protective hairs are replaced. Damp hands, rubber brushes, or fine-toothed combs are not recommended at this time so that the hair is not thinned. Comb only with a short, blunt-toothed comb, and smooth with a brush which is not too soft.

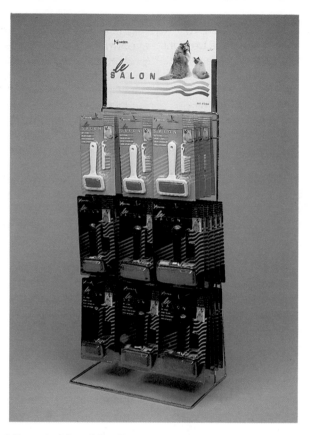

The tightly curled fur of the Rex cats consists only of undercoat type hairs which completely or partially lack the firmer hair types. In caring for such cats, it is sufficient to brush carefully down to the skin.

Longhairs, whose coats are ' brushed with both flowing and upright strokes, require special attention. In contrast to shorthair cats, which, for the most part, do not require such intense care, longhair cats require daily care to

Slicker brushes can help to keep your pet's fur free of mats. Photo courtesy of Hagen.

keep the coat free from knots and matted areas. Such care will keep the coat fluffy and fragrant. In caring for longhair cats, a brush consisting of natural and synthetic bristles, which does not induce static electricity and cause the hair to fly and become knotted, is required along with a special powder. The combs, in two- or three-tooth widths, should be blunt and made of chrome-plated metal. Areas which easily become greasy and matted, such as those behind the ears, base of tail, under the legs and abdomen, are given primary consideration since the cat likes cleaning these areas the least. After powdering, the cat's coat is first combed carefully and without pulling with a wide-toothed comb and then with a finer one to disentangle knots. A brush is then used to remove remaining powder. Special treatment of the back, ruff about the neck, and breast follows. Beginning at the tail, the hair is parted in several places, each area being successively powdered, combed forward, and brushed back. No traces of powder should be allowed to remain in the cat's coat. At shows, the hair of some Persian color varieties is again brushed forward to impart to the cat an especially majestic

Products such as Groom N' Flea Pet Comb make cat-grooming and flea management easy. Photo courtesy of Interplex Labs.

appearance. With other color varieties, it is customary to brush forward only the impressible ruff. The body hair is combed backward with flowing strokes because of its special characteristics. This achieves the desired lustre of the coat.

Longhairs should be familiar with this care from the time they are kittens. Daily care is usually not sufficient during spring when the long underhair is being shed. Special attention is required at the end of summer when the protective hair gradually sheds and has to be removed regularly. The bushy tail sheds last. A longhair is therefore not in a show condition throughout the summer.

Since the hair of a Persian is devoid of natural oils, due to the regular powdering it receives, it can become soaked to the skin in the rain. Therefore, this type of cat is not suitable as an outside cat. If care of its hair is neglected for even a short period of time, eczema can result. This can lead to matting of the hair, which is unpleasant to both cat and keeper. Sometimes only shaving the cat completely can help the skin to heal itself. The cat's hair then only slowly grows back to its full length and beauty.

Bathing is not necessary for healthy housecats, and many of them resist it. There are, however, exceptions, and baths are necessary before shows or in case of disease or parasitic infestation. The following points should be considered when bathing a cat: the cat should not be allowed to slither around in the tub; the water should always be warm; a cat can become very terrified when the shower or faucet is turned on; only a mild children's shampoo or substance prescribed by a veterinarian should be used (never use soaps containing tar products). After bathing, the cat should be dried with towels or placed in a closed basket next to a source of heat. But be careful! It should not get too hot! A loud hairdryer is usually just as loathsome to cats as a noisy vacuum cleaner, although there are exceptions. After a bath a cat should be protected from cold and drafts. There should be a delay of several days between the bath and a show. The hair of a shorthair must once again regain the lustre lost by removal of natural oils, or the cat will appear uncared for and disheveled. The hair of a longhair must be allowed to return to its natural condition and shape without assistance. Hairsprays would be poisonous to the cat!

UNWELCOME GUESTS

Many cats passionately spend their free time lying in wait, capturing and enjoyably devouring flies and mosquitos. This is a doubtful pleasure, since they can become infected with disease-causing germs or poison

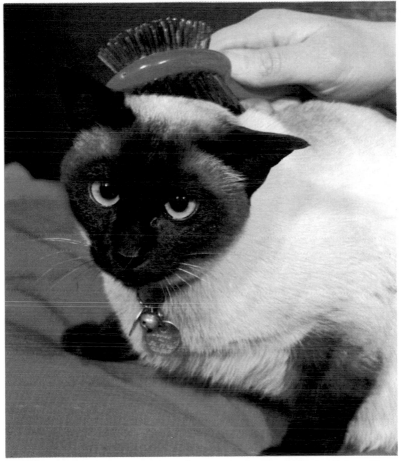

Brushing is an important part of a cat's grooming routine; both shorthair and long-hair cats can benefit from this.

themselves by eating poisoned live prey. Sticky poisonous fly papers, as well as anti-parasitic insecticides, should therefore not be used in the presence of a cat with such hunting ambitions. A further danger exists in a cat's inability to distinguish between flies and other stinging insects; the cat often only becomes wise after an accident. Only the quick intervention of a veterinarian can prevent death by suffocation when, for example, it is stung in the mouth or throat by a wasp.

Ticks can infest a cat even in its own garden. They usually settle on the head or neck and are only first noticed when the cat rubs and scratches itself in an attempt to rid itself of these unwelcome guests. If the ticks are dabbed with a little salad oil, they soon suffocate and can then be carefully removed from the skin. Inflammation may result if the tick's head remains. Ticks are also carriers of various diseases.

It is difficult discovering cat fleas, especially on dark-colored longhairs, since they leave no noticeable traces except for their crumbly excrement. Dog fleas, on the other hand, are easily found, and their bites regularly cause wounds on cats which form scales on the cat's tender skin. They are usually discovered when petting. Both flea varieties rarely affect humans.

Although a carefully tended cat rarely has to suffer from these ectoparasites, it can nonetheless pick up these unpleasant boarders at a show or from a dog living in the same house. Aside from the fact that the cat can seriously scratch itself and become infected from an infestation of fleas, there also exists the greater danger of the cat ingesting a flea and thereby becoming infested with tapeworms. Fleas serve as an intermediate host for these resistant intestinal parasites. When a cat infested with

tapeworms eliminates portions of these worms containing eggs, flea larvae which feed on these eliminated portions become carriers of the eggs. When the larvae develop into full-fledged fleas, they harbor the intermediate stage of the tapeworm with which the cat can re-infect itself as soon as it bites a flea—a vicious cycle indeed! In combatting fleas, the area in proximity to the cat, its bed, blankets, carpets, and spaces between floor boards, should be treated as well as the cat itself. An insecticide harmless to cats, preferably in spray form, should be used. The cat lover should be advised in this regard by a veterinarian, who will be able to recommend the most modern preparations suitable for use on a cat.

Lice or mites are to be suspected when a cat continually scratches and rubs itself without fleas being discovered. Precise determination of what type of parasite is involved can only be made by microscopic means, using hair and skin samples.

Tiny circular bare spots, which gradually spread and begin to heal in the center, although their borders remain red and scaly, may indicate a skin fungus rather than parasites. Laboratory investigation of skin and hair samples can determine if there is a question of ringworm, which is communicable between cats and dogs and infectious to man. If there are several cats living in the household, the healthy cats should be separated from the infected ones according to veterinary instructions. Infections in human beings produce lentil to penny-sized red spots, which should be treated by a dermatologist immediately.

Fungal infections of other types, as well as bacterial infections, can also be determined by a veterinarian, who will initiate successful treatment. The veterinarian should be consulted immediately in all cases involving skin irregularities.

The control of tapeworms, which are primarily caused by fleas, as well as all other intestinal parasites, is carried out under the direction of a veterinarian. An infection of tapeworms is usually only noticed when rice-sized sections of the tapeworm appear in the hair around the cat's anus or in its feces. Intestinal worms such as nematodes, hookworms, and other less frequent types are often only discovered after careful removal and investigation of fecal samples. Intestinal parasites of cats are species-specific and therefore harmless to human beings. Cleanliness and keeping indoors aid in the prevention of

A kitten may seem timid when you first bring it home, but with love and patience, it will soon come to regard your home as its own.

these parasites. A kitten from a good home has already received a careful worming prior to its vaccination against panleukopenia (cat typhoid–distemper). Half a clove of finely cut garlic, which has been squashed in condensed milk and added to the cat's meaty food, is beneficial at monthly intervals. The intestines then become resistant to unwelcome guests of all kinds. Nevertheless, worming the cat should be carried out according to veterinary instructions one or two times a year prior to every vaccination, since worms can seriously affect the cat's health.

CAT CLAWS AND THEIR SIGNIFICANCE

A cat's curved claws, along with their function as weapons, are analogous to human fingers: they enable the cat to securely hold objects of all kinds and to climb skillfully. A free-roaming cat deprived of its curved claw tips by cutting is denied these capabilities. Functioning claws promote a cat's self-confidence.

In nature, a cat enjoys sinking its claws into the coarse bark of a tree and stretching comfortably. This also achieves the removal of the outer horny layer of inefficient claws, exposing the new and usable pointed weapon underneath.

The cat lover can at times find these old claw shells in the scratching post he has placed at his living companion's disposal. A tightly rolled sisal rope fastened under a piece of furniture provides the kitten with a welcome opportunity to work off the energy by training the muscles of its forepaws. At the same time, the kitten will be able to effortlessly shed the old claw shells.

A wide, diagonally positioned board covered with sisal or felt serves the same purpose. Even more interesting, however, is a scratching tree. Fitted with resting places at various levels, it can also serve as a decorative piece of furniture. For longer serviceability, the trunk is tightly wound with thick hemp rope. A climbing post of this kind will be more attractive to a kitten than curtains or upholstered furniture. If your cat does not immediately take to the device but occupies itself elsewhere, clap your hands loudly, saying "No! No!" Admonish the kitten and place it by its scratching post. Thanks to its intelligence, the kitten will get the point very quickly.

EATING HABITS

The opinion is often held that even a housecat must be allowed to tear the meat it is offered, since its four canine teeth have been created for this purpose; this is certainly true for wild cats. The person who has observed his cat while eating sees that it has difficulty in biting large portions into mouth-sized pieces. It can

A male Russian Blue, Katzenburg's Rosko, owned by Ingeborg Urcia.

happen, therefore, that an especially soft or stringy piece of meat will become lodged in the cat's throat; it is only with difficulty that it can be coughed up. Meat should therefore be cut into small pieces before being offered to the cat.

A kitten's set of teeth consists of twenty-six milk teeth, which appear at an age of two to six weeks. The final set of teeth develops from the fourth to seventh month. This set comprises 16 teeth in the upper jaw and 14 in the lower. They should be seen to regularly, and tartar should be removed by the veterinarian.

Cat Grass is a digestive aid specially designed for cats. Photo courtesy of Hagen.

Unlike human beings, it is not necessary for cats to mix their food with saliva. Strong stomach fluids perform all the work for optimal digestion. Undigestible remains are eliminated by eating grass. Sometimes, however, injurious sharp objects nevertheless pass the stomach and intestine and do damage only in the final portion of the intestinal tract. They may block the passage out of the stomach and intestine and debilitate entire portions of the intestine so that only an operation can bring relief.

Eating is an activity which is performed like a ritual by every cat. To this end, it consistently prefers the same quiet place and uses its own clean eating dish. This dish should have a flat bottom and a reasonable high rim

so that nothing can be pushed out. Cats which have become friends have no objection to eating from the same dish. Sick and nursing cats should be brought their food, and the cat lover should give them special attention since they would rather lie where they are than get up. Mother cats often have the habit of copiously massaging the skin and hair of their young with the fat remaining on their tongues from eating. This is only possible if they are given their food where they lie.

Cats take meat into their mouths with the backward pointing horny spurs on their tongues. It is then chewed briefly with the molars before it is swallowed. There are also aesthetes among cats which take meat with their claws and then bring it to their mouths. Purees or liquids are taken up with the tongue as with a spoon. When the cat is satisfied, it leaves a respectable bit behind for later. During the summer months, the leftover morsels should be removed no later than one hour after completion of the meal.

Cats are true gourmets. They occasionally reject tomorrow what pleased them today. What should comprise a cat's meal so that it does not receive too many large portions and become too fat, yet still maintain its appetite, depends largely upon its living habits. Fresh air encourages the appetite, and a lively cat requires more calories than a sluggish one. Pregnant cats usually have a large appetite. They should be fed substantially but with moderation. There is no limitation on feeding nursing cats or growing kittens. A kitten between ten and 20 weeks of age requires three ample meals per day. After the second teeth come in, a small meal in the morning and a main meal in the evening are sufficient. A cat should be observed while eating to determine whether it is enjoying its meals and finds the food pleasing. If the cat declines the food and the addition of yeast or a small amount of salt cannot make it pleasing, sickness due to a clogged nose, injury to the mucus membranes, or digestive disturbances may be the underlying cause of food refusal. Since cats can become emaciated

very quickly, indeed even literally dehydrate when they reject food for an extended period, a veterinarian should be consulted immediately.

Nil-O-Fresh Powdered Rug & Room Deodorizer eliminates strong odors long after vacuuming.

The main portion of every high quality cat diet is meat, to which all else is added (canned food, fish, organ meats). If raw meat has a laxative effect, it should be lightly boiled. To round out a meal, a half-teaspoon of yeast flakes should be spread over the prepared food.

VACCINATIONS

A kitten is protected from infection up to the age of eight or so weeks by antibodies it has received from its mother. The first visit to a veterinarian should take place after this period, so that it may receive its first vaccination against cat typhoid–distemper (panleukopenia). Even today,

numerous free-roaming kittens succumb to this disease. A week prior to this, i.e., at seven weeks of age, it should be wormed under a veterinarian's guidance. However, immunization is only complete when the kitten has withstood the second vaccination at the age of ten weeks. This vaccination is repeated after a year. Older cats can be immunized with a live vaccine which, according to the

A Seal Point Himalayan, Goforth's Monique, and Blue Point Himalayan, Goforth's Blu Moon. Owner, Marguerita Goforth.

A Burmese. Glowing golden eyes are what one first notices about this unique breed of cat.

manufacturers, promises longer protection. There is also a vaccine against certain secondary infections after a cat has a cold (rhinotracheitis), but this is only undertaken by a veterinarian when valid reason exists to fear further infection.

A vaccination against rabies is likewise required prior to a trip abroad. This vaccination is also recommended if there is a possibility of the cat getting outside. A cat outdoors under supervision is thus protected in those areas (endangered by rabies) where free-roaming cats can easily transmit the disease.

Cat Breeding

GENERAL

In most cases, this "hobby" develops into a full-time job for the cat lover, and it occupies not only his leisure time but claims his entire attention. Therefore, everyone who would like to give himself over to this "leisure" occupation should think about the following seven items beforehand:

1) Is your knowledge of heredity in general and of your cat's breed in particular well grounded?
2) Do you have sufficient experience in handling cats?
3) Is the female cat you intend to breed suitable for breeding?
4) Do your household space and family situation guarantee that the kittens will be happily raised?
5) Does your leisure time permit such a taxing occupation, or does your profession allow you enough time for this hobby?
6) Does your wallet permit such an expensive hobby?
7) Are you ready to assume the necessary association with a breeding organization, and all the resulting responsibilities and costs, to procure for your kittens an assured future as purebred cats?

To answer item one with a "yes," the study of genetics is necessary. Item two must, of course, be answered affirmatively, for handling cats, like breeding them, is not an acquired art. A visit to a cat show is indispensable to answer item three. The answer to item seven is the result of this visit. To be able to visit a show, the cat lover should have already approached a breeding organization, if he has not already joined it. All these breeding organizations produce pedigrees for cats bred by their members, which are often designated as family trees, proof of bloodline, or genealogical tables. The organizations often allow the evaluation of their purebred cats and offspring to be undertaken at shows by international judges. Item four likewise requires further explanation. In order to raise its offspring, a cat requires as much room as possible in which it can find rest as well as take part in family activities. A household with several small children, therefore, usually does not offer space for a kitten nursery. An apartment which is too small does not offer kittens sufficient opportunity for the play and movement they need. They must not, however, have the opportunity to fall victim to a household accident. Walls, floors,

Facing page: Cats are very inquisitive and like to look out of the window. Note the keenness of expression on the face of this black-and-white longhair.

and furniture should be easy to clean and disinfect; curtains and upholstered furniture should not be too delicate. Generosity and almost stoic calmness is necessary in raising kittens.

Even item five requires a more thorough look before an answer is possible. If the cat lover does not have a profession which assures a generous vacation, then cat breeding is not for him, even if keeping a cat is absolutely satisfactory. It must be possible to remain away from work when, for example, the prospective mother prepares to deliver, or when kittens must be fed every two hours, day and night, because something has happened to the mother. The cat lover must be able to provide food regularly to the cat family and be able to observe them during meals.

Item six indicates that breeding cats is not suitable as a bread-winning occupation. Cat breeding is and remains a true hobby according to the motto: "A hobby horse eats more than a hundred work horses." Whoever thinks he knows better will sooner or later learn from experience that he has made a mistake. Cats cannot be fed cheaply. One cannot skimp either in breeding or keeping cats. Cats require evenly heated rooms and, because of the vaccinations alone, the regular and costly care of a veterinarian. If the cat lover does not possess the means to allow generous expenditures for

his hobby, it would be better if he did not begin at all. Consequently, item seven would also be answered negatively. Everything which is considered with belonging to an association, such as dues, shows, booth registration, mating the female, and pedigree, is coupled, in part, with considerable expenditures.

If even one of the questions posed cannot be answered with an unequivocal "yes," a responsible cat lover should, for his cat's sake as well as his own, reconsider his intention to breed cats.

THE STUD CAT

Many keepers of studs are very generous and tolerant, and they live with these cats despite their burdensome habits, while others banish them to their own areas with a cat run and all the cat comforts which they share with others of their species. Sometimes male cats give up on demonstrations of their masculinity as soon as they realize there is no female cat ready to mate for miles around. Usually, however, they do not stop marking their area with scent. Although many male cats would probably make excellent fathers, they should not be allowed to live in immediate proximity to female cats, because in no case should there be unwanted and unplanned offspring. Studs should also be kept separated from other mature male cats, since they are rivals and can become involved in heated fights which can cause serious injury.

Keeping male breeding cats therefore presents difficulties. Even if male cats know each other for a long time, they still do not

Keystone Juniper, red and-white pregnant female Persian, in her maternity box. Owner, Marianne Lawrence.

miss an opportunity to fight. If one of the two is castrated, the fighting spirit of the other sometimes gradually diminishes because of the lack of enthusiasm of the castrate.

Every cat lover can, by consulting show catalogs and advertisements, choose a first-class, suitable partner for his female cat. Because of the problems in keeping a breeding

male, a fee for its services is set in advance.

It is most advantageous to compare the pedigrees of the two future partners. Good breeding results are often to be expected when both indicate some corresponding outstanding ancestors. These results are due to hidden (recessive) inheritable traits, becoming visible in the offspring only when they appear in the lineage of both parents. Indeed, this is true for desirable as well as undesirable traits. Another good way to find a suitable partner is to carefully look at the offspring of your chosen male with various female cats and to observantly follow their evaluation at shows. In addition, the male cat should, as much as possible, possess to perfection all those features (type, quality of fur, gentle character, etc.) lacking in the female. In any event, the mating plans proceed as with true royalty. In this connection, the cat lover should take care that the future "groom" for his "little bride" belongs to the same breeding association as his female (and himself), so that the offspring later receive the pedigree due them.

An Abyssinian. Champion Nepenthes Akime at ten months of age. Owners, Joan and Alfred Wastlhuber.

Proper diet, regular veterinary care, and exercise are important factors in your pet's health.

THE FEMALE BREEDING CAT OR QUEEN

Every cat lover will now realize that only a first-class female with the best characteristics of its breed can be suited as a breeding cat, if the offspring is to later win under its own name. In addition, the female cat should possess an even, peaceful nature and really be drawn to humans. It is a true, gently reigning queen.

A female cat which is intended for breeding and rearing of young is given neither the pill nor hormone injections to suppress its longing for a male. The reproductive organs of the cat are so delicate in their combined action that intervention of any kind can contribute to longlasting breeding failures. A cat should not be allowed to become a mother until it is at least one year old. Its system must be allowed to mature. For this reason, even the second estrus is questionable as the earliest fixed period for mating. One can in good conscience wait longer with some of the delicate breeds. It would be best to seek the advice of a veterinarian, should a very delicate cat suffer from frequent periods of estrus when mating is not yet be desired.

Before mating, the female should be tested for worms and once again vaccinated against cat-typhoid–distemper. Then, when estrus begins, an appointment is made with the keeper of the breeding male. The female should be placed with its partner on the third day.

During the trip, the female is transported in its carrier and spends most of the trip meowing. Upon its arrival at the male's residence (it should not encounter any strange females there), it begins to feel well and secure. After the female sits opposite its chosen mate, separated by the mesh doors of its cage at first, it soon forgets the discomforts of the journey.

The responsible breeder sees to it that a female raises at most only three litters in two years so that she remains well and resistant to disease. If one possesses two friendly females which are capable of mating, it is advisable to set the period between births such that the owner can devote himself intensively to the rearing of each litter. Ideally, this means that the first litter has already left the house at the age of approximately 12 weeks before the litter of the second female is born. Experience shows that other arrangements will certainly lead to stress situations for all participants, and

why shouldn't this be avoided?

MATING

The experienced male cat immediately knows who is approaching when an occupied transport cage is placed in his area. Therefore, a female cat that is to be mated for the first time is, if possible, entrusted to an experienced partner. Conversely, a male cat that is to be mated for the first time is best associated with an experienced female that does not seriously resent the initial aggression meant for supposed rivals.

The stud cat at first begins to entice the female with cooing sounds while she cowers, full of tension and fear, in her carrier. If the male cautiously nears the mesh door, the female will swipe or hiss at him. The door is opened a bit only after the female has become calm and begins to take note of his courting. When the female feels courageous, she will carefully come out, and the male will then nimbly slip inside to assimilate the female's exciting fragrance. After a while, the male appears at the door with a dazed look, upper lip drawn up, simultaneously surprised and enchanted. The male also looks toward his partner, which, in the meantime, has begun to thoroughly inspect corners, resting places, and litter boxes with the same facial expression. The male then follows the female to capture

A chinchilla Persian dam with her three-week-old kittens.

CAT BREEDING

more of its fragrance.

At this time the female appears to regard this intimate approach as annoying. A ritual according to strict instinctive laws is now performed, and this is similar to the one performed when cats become acquainted. The male now marks various strategic, important spots in the area to convince the female of his qualities and attempts not to overstep the set flight distance while constantly offering tender enticements. The female cleverly avoids him. If the male approaches and perhaps springs upon her back from above in a sudden surprise attack to grasp her about the nape, she will strike back and hiss. If the male lands softly on her back, the female will shriek shrilly, turn around, and send him into flight. This coquettish game is repeated in all phases with every mating of cats, unless the two partners know each other for a long time or are an intimate mated pair. The length of the cage is dependant upon so many various conditions that the cat lover can only wait patiently to see what happens. The best thing for the cat lover to do is to leave without his companion and request the keeper of the male to let him know when the cats have consumated the mating.

On the following night, the loud, piercing cry of the female usually announces that the male has achieved his goal and subdued her. After every move of the male, the female turns toward him and attempts to strike him with lightning quick swipes of her paws. The male adroitly avoids her and sits in a corner licking itself, evidently somewhat perplexed. Meanwhile, the female rolls about wildly on the floor and then finally cleans herself.

This procedure repeats itself several times. Appetite is greatly diminished in both cats during the entire period, and they hardly touch the foods offered to them. Hunger appears after one or two days, when mutual interest diminishes. The female often attempts to once again excite her partner by rolling and meowing loudly. Sometimes both crouch in different corners exhausted or behave like dear friends by pawing each other. As soon as either of the partners seeks to leave the room when the door is opened, it is time to separate them.

The keeper of the female pays the fee agreed upon immediately after a consumated mating. If the female has not conceived, she will once again go into heat after three weeks or so. Another mating attempt will usually be granted for free. The keeper of the male issues a receipt, which is required for the future registration of the offspring in the breeding book of the appropriate association. A male cat goes to the home of the female for breeding purposes only in exceptional circumstances, and in such cases, must be left sufficient time to take in his new surroundings and appropriately mark them with his scent. The male is allowed to make contact with the ready female only after this procedure and then again only with the female in her transport cage. A small distinctly arranged room, such as a bathroom with tiled walls that are easily cleaned,

For a kitten, playtime with its mother and its littermates is a pleasurable—and necessary—activity.

is best suited as a mating room. The items for the room consist of a litter box, water dishes, and a small carpet. In the event the proper mating time is missed, mating should be postponed until the next estrus of the female. A female cat that is no longer willing to mate may simply shut herself off so that even the most ardent cooing of the male is entirely in vain.

A Siamese. Champion Suzzi's Rembrandt of Velvet Paws, a Chocolate Point male. Owners, Doris and Bill Thoms.

PREGNANCY

After the cat lover returns home with his companion, he naturally expects her period of estrus to have passed and nine peaceful weeks to begin. However, he is deluding himself. After a brief pause of several hours to catch her breath, the female once again begins to roll about and, when petted on the back, raises her tail to the side in a mating gesture. On no account must the female be allowed to come in contact with another male during this period. The possibility exists that several days after a successful mating, the female may mate with another male. The consequences would be a mixed litter of kittens from different fathers which are in widely varying stages of development and naturally without legitimate claim to pedigrees. Estrus usually ends after two to three days. The female has conceived if, after three weeks, the lower of the four or five pairs of teats on its stomach begin to turn a soft pink. The length of pregnancy varies among the different breeds. Among Siamese, Oriental Shorthairs, and the medium-built cat breeds the gestation is approximately nine complete weeks and two days (65 days) from the first day of mating. Sixty-three days are taken as the basis for determining delivery dates. Sometimes the pregnancy lasts 67 or even 69 days. This should be no cause for concern.

Many cat fanciers consider the cat to be the cleanest domestic animal known to man.

Among Persians and other longhairs the pregnancy usually lasts 63 to 65 days. Domestic Shorthairs occasionally have shorter pregnancies.

A healthy female cat does not require special attention during pregnancy except for plenty of fresh air (well-aired rooms, use of cat run in good weather). It usually feels well and content and passes the greater portion of the time away incubating its young. The female sometimes becomes mildly impatient with other cats that it gladly had around it before. This behavior begins about ten days before the expected delivery and then because the queen is on the lookout for a substitute child on which it can exercise its incipient motherly instinct of grooming and cleaning.

FALSE PREGNANCY AND MISCARRIAGE

A female cat can imagine a pregnancy. All signs, in fact, indicate that it is expecting: the teats become red and they begin to increase noticeably in size, but nothing happens. Labor pains begin on the calculated delivery day, but there are no kittens. The first estrus follows approximately three weeks later. Prior to this, the female cares for its substitute child, if available, but now she vigorously seeks a male.

Such a pregnancy, however, is frequently not only imagined. A mating has actually taken place and the development of the embryos began in the mother's body, but from a certain point on faulty hormonal regulation prevented their further development. A degeneration and assimilation took place in the mother's body. This can frequently be observed in females which have taken the pill or received hormone injections and were then mated on the following estrus. It is better to let this estrus pass and

only permit mating afterwards. Even if this method does not always guarantee normal pregnancies later, it certainly helps. Nevertheless, there must be continued emphatic warnings against the use of hormone preparations in female breeding cats.

SEEKING A PLACE TO GIVE BIRTH

During the last four weeks of a pregnancy, most female cats begin to look around for a suitable shelter in which to give birth. The cat lover can observe his pet rummaging around in cabinets and drawers and endlessly digging up blankets and pillows whenever it has the oppurtunity. Now and again it tries out the comfortable mess it has made, but soon gets up dissatisfied and seeks new and better possibilities. At this point, the cat lover can offer the basket or box he has intended as the delivery bed, but this should at first contain only pillows or blankets and not the material intended for the birth, since everything would have to once again be washed and cleaned before delivery of the kittens.

Place the delivery bed in its final quarters, if possible. Choosing this place should be planned with foresight. The cat lover will only torture himself if he chooses, for example, a slightly opened cupboard as the place of birth.

A Himalayan, Copplestone Maria, owned by I. Bentinck.

When it is finally the cat's time, hours upon hours will pass in which the cat lover will have to crouch in front of the cupboard in order to assist his companion. It is better, therefore, to choose a couch or a low, broad, small table. The cat lover can then rest nearby if the waiting period lasts too long. A strong, roomy cardboard carton, open at the top, can be chosen as a bed in which the cat can stretch out and brace itself with its paws on the opposite sides. Such a bed is ideal if the cat can comfortably get in and out during the last days of pregnancy. The small side of the carton can be folded down to facilitate this, and it can later be raised and secured. A wooden kittening box with removable lid

and round entrance is recommended in some breeding circles. Some people contend that a new cardboard carton is more appropriate as a delivery bed for hygienic reasons.

The chosen bed should be thoroughly cleaned, disinfected, and dried in the sun, if possible, before it is used for its intended purpose. Even a basket, a den which female cats seem to prefer above all others, should be given a thorough cleaning before it is used. This delivery bed should have as wide a bottom area as possible and a large round entrance to permit the cat lover trouble-free management and observation of all events within. The temperature inside such a bed can be satisfactorily regulated by means of a light blanket draped over the top or by means of a heating pad, at its lowest setting, placed either in front of the entrance or fastened to the side. The queen can observe all happenings taking place in its surroundings, even though it is in the quietest corner of the room out of the mainstream of events.

THE GREAT EVENT

It is advisable to make the veterinarian aware of the approaching delivery a few days prior to the day you have calculated. A situation may possibly arise which requires his help at an unusual time; he should be prepared.

The weight of the expectant mother increases evenly up to the time of delivery. The movement of the young in the womb, which is noticeable from the fifth week of pregnancy, can be clearly observed on both sides of its body. As delivery time approaches, it appears as if the weight has shifted to the rear. The female cat follows its keeper everywhere. It would be best for the cat lover to rest evenings in the cat's vicinity so that he can be near its side when it needs him. The hair on the stomach of longhair cats can be clipped, both to keep it from becoming dirty and matted and to make the teats more accessible to the young. It is not necessary to wash and

disinfect their teats as is often recommended. The acidic covering of the skin, which offers protection from infection, can easily be destroyed by too much human cleaning. The female cat best takes care of its own cleaning. It is important that the bed be kept meticulously clean. If inflammations or painful swellings appear, seek veterinary advice immediately. Practical treatment depends on his advice only.

Padding the delivery bed is accomplished with a light cotton blanket and a layer of soft, boilable, clean cloth which can be quickly changed as the need arises. A heating pad should be at hand. Anything which may be needed in the coming hours should be on a small table and easily accessible. This includes a bundle of thin cloths, several packets of tissues, a few small washcloths, petroleum jelly, surgical scissors (bent tips, both blunt), 70% alcohol solution to disinfect scissors, a large basin (with lid) with boiled water to which a disinfectant must be added for hand washing, a small pail with a lid (for used cloths, etc.), writing material, and an accurate scale.

The first sure sign of labor pains in cats is a loss of appetite, but there are exceptions. The female cat lies down on its bed purring loudly and deeply when the first contractions are evident. At this time a little mucus appears at her rear. If the female has lived in close association with another cat, it will insist that this one remain near it to massage her sides with its tongue. This cat must also lick the stomach and knead it with its paws. This midwifery helps in encouraging contractions. As the period between contractions gradually diminishes, the first kitten is pushed out from one of the uterine branches. A sudden flood of almost colorless amniotic fluid indicates that the kitten is on its way. Every cat appreciates cheering and comforting encouragement, since the birth of the first kitten is usually very painful and slow. A transparent bubble soon appears at the vaginal orifice. This is part of the fetal envelope which surrounds the kitten. The first kitten is usually born head first after an especially strong contraction, which is sometimes coupled by a cry from the cat.

A brown tabby longhair.

The veterinarian is to be advised immediately, however, if the kitten's tail, paws, or both appear after release of the amniotic fluid and appearance of the amniotic sac (breech birth). This is important if, after a few contractions, no progress is noted and the kitten cannot be removed during a contraction by a gentle pull with tissue-covered hands. The cat should be comforted until the veterinarian appears to diminish contractions and pressure from the kitten. The amniotic sac is gently pushed back with a lubricated finger until the veterinarian arrives.

A young queen giving birth for the first time is often so shaken that it attempts to run away. It should be gently restrained. If the female does not immediately begin to lick the kitten's face, the cat lover can help by carefully ripping open the amniotic sac over the kitten's head with his index finger to free its nose. The kitten's nose should then be carefully wiped clean with a tissue. The kitten is connected to the placenta (afterbirth) by means of a long umbilical cord from which it has received oxygen and other nourishment up to the time of its birth. For the first time, the kitten

An Abyssinian, Champion Nepenthes Leo, owned by Joan and Alfred Wastlhuber.

is forced to use its lungs to breathe when the mother eats the afterbirth and severs the umbilical cord.

Things, however, do not always proceed in this manner. It often happens that the kitten is born and the umbilical cord breaks without the appearance of the afterbirth. The female sometimes does not care at all about what is happening and acts totally helpless. The cat lover must intervene in these cases. He massages the umbilical cord in the direction of the newly born kitten until it is emptied of blood. Using the sterilized surgical scissors, the umbilical cord is then severed approximately six inches from the kitten's stomach. The small remaining portion of the umbilical cord dries up within a few hours, and it eventually falls off by itself after a few days.

If the mother does not lick and clean its young itself, take a coarse terry cloth and dry the kitten well with gentle, circular patting movements while pointing its head downwards. This allows the remains of mucus and amniotic fluid to drain from the breathing passages. Artificial respiration should not be attempted, so that remaining fluids do not enter the breathing passages. It would be appropriate to gently shake the kitten. Take care to support the nape of the neck with the index finger while shaking. At the first squeaking sound, weigh the kitten quickly and return it to its mother's care. The female will now attend to it as much as the progress of the delivery will allow.

It is advantageous to take the minutes of the delivery, writing down the entire proceeding, including precise time and weight information. It is important at this point to make note of the afterbirth that is still missing. If it appears after the second or third kitten, it is then known that it belonged to the first and that there exists no cause for concern. No afterbirth should be unaccounted for after completion of delivery, since it can cause fever and other complications.

AFTER THE DELIVERY

Immediately after completion of delivery, the cat lover should ascertain whether or not all afterbirths have been accounted for. A placenta which is still missing may appear when contractions are induced by stroking. If this does not help, the veterinarian will have to administer a labor-inducing injection.

A female cat usually knows best when all kittens have been born. The cat lover can be deceived by feeling the body, since the kidneys can be easily mistaken for unborn kittens. The mother cat now lies purring contentedly and happily near its young, which are sating themselves on her well-filled teats. Whether one of these is producing enough milk can be determined by pressing at its base and then pulling gently at its tip. A drop of the milk should appear. This colostrum is of especially great value since, along with a high protein, vitamin, and mineral content, it contains the mother's antibodies which protect the kitten from certain diseases, primarily during the first week of life. Kittens are more susceptible to illnesses when this milk is lacking.

Determining the kitten's sex is generally easiest immediately after birth. In female kittens, the anus and vagina are near each other and the tiny vulva can already be recognized easily. Sex is easily determined in a litter of mixed sexes, since a comparison can be made.

Even the color of the kittens is

Above: *Blotched silver tabby British Shorthair.* **Facing page, top:** *The established housecat is put off by the smell of the newcomer who submits to a scent-examination.* **Facing page, bottom:** *These uniformly developed smoke Persian kittens must, from six weeks of age onward, be regularly brushed.*

readily discernible. Stripes and spots already show their future form and extent. A hereditary kink of the tail is more evident now than it will be a few days or weeks later. Siamese are born snow white, and brown Burmese café au lait. The fur of all kittens is soft and woolly. Siamese and Oriental Shorthairs have the shortest baby fur, while the fur of the Persian is especially compact and appears twice as dense. Since kittens are born blind, the color of the eyes cannot yet be determined.

LITTER ANNOUNCEMENTS

At least three weeks should elapse before the cat lover submits a litter announcement to his breeding association; this precludes an incorrect report. This report contains information regarding sex, color, and names of the kittens. Six to eight weeks must pass before the cat lover is able to report the final colors of Siamese markings precisely.

The opportunity should be taken to completely change the bedding in the kittening box with fresh cloths the first time the mother leaves it. When lifting the young, use both hands. It is astonishing that the kittens already hiss and spit loudly to terrify the enemy. Bed changing should take place daily during the first week, otherwise many mother cats will seek a cleaner place for their families, even if it is the nearest piece of upholstered furniture.

COMPLICATIONS AND SUBSTITUTE MOTHERING

A veterinarian's quick intervention is necessary should a female cat have difficulty bringing its young into the world. Something is wrong if there is no progress one half-hour after release of the amniotic fluid, if the cat sits in its bed and cries, becomes nervous and desperate, or attempts to run around. There may be a question of weakness caused by labor, abnormal position of the kitten (e.g., transverse position), or too narrow a pelvis, etc. The emergency measures taken depend on the veterinarian's diagnosis (labor-inducing injection, turning the kitten in the mother's body, or Caesarean delivery).

Rigid or distorted limbs in a kitten can be the consequence of an unfortunate position in the mother's body. Veterinary advice is recommended if this deformity does not disappear within two or three days. The same is true for all deformities, even when they are not immediately recognizable, such as cleft palate. A mother cat will usually instinctively decline rearing a kitten incapable of living and will remove it from the litter or refuse to nurse it. Kittens with internal deformities often fail to find the mother's teats and lie off to the side while the others nurse. On the other hand, if a kitten is too weak to nurse because of a troublesome birth, it is usually helpful to carefully administer a few drops of milk solution (1:4) with a dropper. The kitten should not be placed on its back but should be allowed to suck by itself. Afterwards, it will often find its mother's teats and will join the others. The mother and kittens should be left only when all the young are nursing normally.

The word round *is frequently used to describe the Persian, particularly the head.*

Blue Lynx Point Siamese with vivid blue eye color. In Europe, Lynx Points are called Tabby Points.

The Burmese, in comparison to the Siamese pictured on the facing page, is of different body type (medium-slender as opposed to the svelte foreign type required of the Siamese) and has a rounder head than the typey wedge-shaped head of the Siamese.

A veterinarian should be consulted in all cases where putting one of the kittens to sleep is unavoidable. He will perform the task quickly and painlessly by means of an injection. Under no circumstances should the cat lover attempt any other means of destroying a kitten.

Kittens which are born dead of unknown causes or die in the first few days (fading kittens) should be sent without delay to the nearest investigative laboratory of veterinary medicine to determine the cause of death and preclude similar cases in the future.

A substitute mother should be sought whenever kittens lose their natural one. If inquiries of the veterinarian, other breeders, etc., cannot produce a substitute nurser, spays may be considered, since the mother instinct is very strong in almost all cats. They will keep the kittens warm, clean and will massage them; they may only not be able to give milk.

Unfortunately, substitute mothering is difficult. Because the kittens lack the mother's colostrum, they do not receive the important disease antibodies found in it. Despite all efforts, they sometimes do not live. Substitute mothering without the assistance of another cat promises even less hope of success, since a human being cannot perform necessary tasks, such as the required massaging of the stomach necessary for proper digestion

that a cat would. If the cat lover wishes to attempt rearing orphaned kittens, he must regularly provide for them every two hours, day and night, during the first week and every four hours the following week. Nighttime meals can be dispensed with from the third week on.

Commercial cat-milk preparations are available which are suitable for rearing the kittens. The cat lover should follow the instructions of the milk preparation he intends to use. The milk should always be given at body temperature. The kitten should be fed in a normal position, not lying on its back. It will grasp the tiny ball of the pipette with its tongue and suck by itself. Choking, and the attendant possibility of fluids getting into the breathing passages (causing lung inflammation), are thereby avoided. Syringes used in administering fluids to larger cats are not suitable due to their short tips. A special nursing bottle can be used instead of the ball pipette. All utensils must be kept scrupulously clean and germ-free by boiling.

By the third week of the kittens' life, approximately six meals a day are necessary. It is necessary to replace the orphaned kittens' in-between meals, which are not forthcoming from the mother's teats, with commercial cat-milk.

If the cat lover must care for the orphaned kittens without any

The coat of the Somali is medium long and therefore relatively easy to care for.

Facing page, top: *Cats care for their claws themselves. A slanted scratchboard such as this one helps them with this activity.* Facing page, bottom: *An ebony Oriental Shorthair kitten.* Above: *A blue Oriental Shorthair. Cat breeding should not be left to chance. Unsupervised, a cat can get loose outside and get lost or could mate freely with a cat of whatever breed it comes into contact with.*

assistance from another cat, he should massage their abdomens with a soft terry cloth that has been moistened with oil, after every meal. The kittens' wet behinds are afterwards dabbed with a tissue, or cleaned with a wad of cotton and warm water, and then carefully dried. Even the kittens' baby fur requires regular care. This should be stroked against the grain with a soft brush.

The kittens should never be allowed to lie directly on a heating pad. For this reason, it is better to fasten it in a hanging position alongside their bed. Always keep a heating pad at its lowest setting. This way they can draw nearer or further away at will and still enjoy the necessary even warmth which they would otherwise get from their mother.

At the age of 11 weeks, the time has come for the first seriously interested party to turn up to take one of the kittens home. The cat lover should always attempt to keep in touch with the kittens' new keeper. Only in this way will he be able to intervene in a helpful manner when unforeseen problems need to be solved. The cat lover will often be the only one able to give proper advice from his precise knowledge of every individual kitten, even if it is only a question of recommending a good veterinarian who knows his way with cats. In this way he comes to realize the happy feeling a healthy, carefully raised kitten can bring to its new keeper.

A rubber ball is one of many toys that your cat will enjoy playing with.

Index

Overleaf: In general, cats—no matter what their breed—are inquisitive creatures.

CAT CARE
KW-064